How to Unlock the Heart of Genuine Human Connection

Master the Conversations That Spark Deeper
Relationships, Build Trust, and Unlock
Meaningful Communication

Pet Biggie

1

Table of Content

Introduction

The Art of Genuine Human Connection

In a world that often feels increasingly disconnected despite our digital interconnectedness, the art of genuine human connection stands as a beacon of hope and fulfillment. Imagine a world where every conversation you have is not just an exchange of words but a dance of souls, a symphony of emotions, and a meeting of minds. This is the essence of true connection, where communication transcends the mundane and touches the very core of our being. As an emotional philosopher, I invite you to embark on a journey that will unlock the heart of meaningful communication and enrich every interaction you have.

The Superpower of Effective Communication

Effective communication is nothing short of a superpower. It is the golden thread that weaves the fabric of our relationships, professional engagements, and even our self-understanding. When wielded with skill and intention, communication can build bridges, heal wounds, and create profound bonds that withstand the tests of time and adversity. It is through our words and the emotions they convey that we influence others, inspire change, and leave an indelible mark on the world.

Consider for a moment the times you have felt truly understood, when someone listened to you with their heart as much as their ears. These moments are rare and precious, often standing out in our memories like beacons of light in the darkness. This is the power of effective communication – the ability to make others feel seen, heard, and valued. It is not merely about transmitting information but about fostering a shared human experience.

Effective communication requires us to be present, to engage with empathy, and to approach every conversation with an open heart and mind. It is about tuning into the unspoken words, the subtle cues, and the underlying emotions that give depth and meaning to our interactions. In mastering this art, we become more than just speakers and listeners; we become connectors, healers, and creators of authentic human bonds.

Understanding the Layers of Conversation

To truly master the art of genuine human connection, it is essential to understand that every conversation operates on three distinct layers: practical, emotional, and social.

Each layer plays a crucial role in shaping the dynamics of our interactions and the quality of our relationships.

The practical layer is the surface level of conversation. It involves the exchange of information, ideas, and facts. This is where we discuss plans, share updates, and convey instructions. While practical conversations are necessary for day-to-day functioning, they often lack the depth needed to foster genuine connection. However, mastering this layer is the foundation upon which deeper layers are built.

Beneath the practical layer lies the emotional layer. This is where our feelings, desires, and vulnerabilities come into play. Emotional conversations are rich and complex, filled with the nuances of our inner experiences. They require us to be open and honest, to share not just what we think but what we feel. Engaging at this level allows us to connect on a more intimate and personal level, fostering empathy and understanding.

The deepest layer is the social layer, which encompasses the broader context of our interactions. This includes the social norms, cultural influences, and relational dynamics that shape how we communicate. Understanding this layer involves recognizing the roles we play in different settings, the expectations placed upon us, and the unspoken rules that govern our behavior. Mastering the social layer allows us to navigate complex social landscapes with grace and adaptability.

By recognizing and skillfully navigating these layers, we can create conversations that are not only meaningful but transformative. We can move beyond superficial exchanges to build connections that are deeply rooted in understanding and mutual respect. This book will guide you through each layer, providing insights and techniques to enhance your communication skills and deepen your relationships.

Why This Book Matters

In an era where digital communication often replaces face-to-face interactions, the art of genuine human connection has never been more important. This book matters because it addresses a fundamental human need – the need to connect, to belong, and to be understood. It offers a roadmap to mastering the conversations that can spark deeper relationships, build trust, and unlock meaningful communication.

This book is not just about improving your social skills; it is about transforming your approach to communication in every aspect of your life. Whether you are looking to strengthen personal relationships, enhance professional collaborations, or simply become a more effective communicator, the principles and practices outlined in these pages will provide you with the tools you need.

Through the stories, examples, and exercises included in this book, you will learn how to navigate complex emotions, negotiate differing beliefs, and connect with others on a deeper level. You will discover how to recognize and match the layers of conversation, fostering interactions that are not only effective but also enriching.

In essence, this book is a journey towards becoming a master of communication – someone who can unlock the heart of genuine human connection and create relationships that are truly meaningful. It is an invitation to step into your power as a communicator, to embrace the beauty of human connection, and to transform the way you interact with the world around you.

By investing in this journey, you are not only enhancing your ability to connect with others but also enriching your own life. The skills you will develop through this book will empower you to navigate life's challenges with confidence and grace, fostering relationships that bring joy, fulfillment, and a sense of belonging. So, let's embark on this transformative journey together and unlock the true power of effective communication.

It is important to recognize that the journey towards mastering genuine human connection is a lifelong one. It is a journey filled with growth, discovery, and the occasional misstep. But it is also a journey that promises profound rewards – the kind of rewards that come from building deep, meaningful relationships and creating a positive impact on the lives of others.

Effective communication is a skill that can be learned and perfected. It is a superpower that, once unlocked, has the potential to transform every aspect of your life. By understanding and mastering the layers of conversation, you can create connections that are not only effective but also deeply enriching.

This book is your guide on this journey. It offers insights, techniques, and practical exercises to help you develop the skills needed to become a master communicator. It invites you to explore the art of genuine human connection and to embrace the power of effective communication.

So, as we embark on this journey together, remember that every conversation is an opportunity – an opportunity to connect, to understand, and to be understood. Embrace this journey with an open heart and a curious mind, and you will discover the profound beauty of genuine human connection.

Chapter 1

The Foundations of Human Connection

The Three Layers of Conversation: Practical, Emotional, Social

Conversations are the building blocks of human relationships, the threads that weave the tapestry of our social fabric. They are not merely exchanges of words but complex interactions that involve layers of meaning and emotion. To understand the true art of communication, one must first grasp the three fundamental layers of conversation: practical, emotional, and social.

The Practical Layer

The practical layer is the surface level of communication. It is straightforward and factual, involving the exchange of information, instructions, and ideas. This is the realm of everyday logistics—coordinating schedules, sharing updates, discussing plans. Practical conversations are essential for functioning in our daily lives. They keep us organized, informed, and connected on a basic level.

However, practical conversations, while necessary, often lack depth. They can be transactional, serving a clear purpose but not necessarily building a deeper connection. Yet, mastering the practical layer is the foundation upon which deeper, more meaningful interactions are built. Clear, concise, and effective communication in this layer ensures that misunderstandings are minimized and that the flow of information is smooth.

The Emotional Layer

Beneath the practical layer lies the emotional layer. This is where conversations take on a richer, more complex dimension. Emotional conversations are imbued with feelings, desires, and vulnerabilities. They involve sharing our inner experiences, expressing our needs, and responding to the emotions of others. Engaging at this level requires openness and empathy.

Emotional conversations are the lifeblood of meaningful relationships. They allow us to connect on a human level, to understand and be understood in our full emotional complexity. When we share our joys, fears, hopes, and disappointments, we invite others into our inner world. This creates intimacy and trust, the cornerstones of deep, lasting relationships. However, navigating the emotional layer requires skill and sensitivity. It involves active listening, empathy, and the ability to respond to emotions without judgment.

The Social Layer

The deepest layer is the social layer, encompassing the broader context of our interactions. This includes the social norms, cultural influences, and relational dynamics that shape how we communicate. Understanding this layer involves recognizing the roles we play in different settings, the expectations placed upon us, and the unspoken rules that govern our behavior.

Social conversations are about navigating the complex web of human relationships. They involve understanding the context in which communication takes place, adapting our communication style to fit that context, and managing the social dynamics that influence interactions. This layer is particularly important in professional and social settings, where the ability to navigate social dynamics can significantly impact our success and well-being.

By recognizing and skillfully navigating these layers, we can create conversations that are not only meaningful but transformative. We can move beyond superficial exchanges to build connections that are deeply rooted in understanding and mutual respect.

How Conversations Shape Relationships

Conversations are the lifelines of our relationships. They shape the way we connect with others, influence our perceptions, and build or break trust. Every interaction, whether casual or profound, contributes to the tapestry of our relationships, weaving threads of connection that define our social world.

Building Trust and Intimacy

Trust is the bedrock of any meaningful relationship, and it is built one conversation at a time. When we engage in open, honest dialogue, we demonstrate vulnerability and authenticity. This openness invites reciprocity, encouraging others to share their own truths and vulnerabilities. Over time, these exchanges create a foundation of trust and intimacy.

Consider the relationships in your life that are built on trust. Reflect on the conversations that have fostered this trust. These are likely marked by honesty, empathy, and mutual respect. They involve listening without judgment, validating each other's experiences, and responding with care and understanding. Trust grows in these moments, creating a bond that can withstand challenges and conflicts.

Influencing Perceptions and Emotions

Conversations have the power to shape our perceptions and emotions. The words we choose, the tone we use, and the emotions we convey can all influence how others perceive us and how they feel in our presence. Positive, uplifting conversations can create feelings of joy, connection, and affirmation. Conversely, negative or critical conversations can evoke feelings of hurt, frustration, and disconnection.

Understanding this influence allows us to be more mindful in our interactions. By choosing our words with care, responding with empathy, and striving to understand others' perspectives, we can create conversations that uplift and connect. This mindful approach to communication can transform our relationships, making them sources of joy and support.

Navigating Conflicts and Differences

Conflict is an inevitable part of any relationship. However, the way we navigate these conflicts can either strengthen or weaken our bonds. Constructive conversations can turn conflicts into opportunities for growth and understanding. This involves approaching conflicts with an open mind, seeking to understand the other person's perspective, and working collaboratively to find solutions.

Effective conflict resolution requires emotional intelligence and communication skills. It involves managing our own emotions, listening actively to the other person, and expressing our needs and concerns in a respectful manner. When we navigate conflicts with empathy and a focus on resolution, we build resilience in our relationships, creating a stronger, more connected bond.

Creating Shared Meaning and Purpose

Conversations are also a way to create shared meaning and purpose in our relationships. Through dialogue, we can explore our values, goals, and dreams, finding common ground and building a shared vision for the future. This shared purpose can be a powerful source of connection and motivation, deepening our relationships and giving them a sense of direction and meaning.

Consider the conversations that have defined your most meaningful relationships. These are likely marked by a sense of shared purpose, where you and the other person have explored your values and aspirations together. These conversations create a sense of unity and alignment, fostering a deeper connection and commitment.

The Science Behind Human Connection

Understanding the science behind human connection can deepen our appreciation for the complexity and beauty of our social interactions. Research from fields such as psychology, neuroscience, and sociology provides valuable insights into the mechanisms that drive our need for connection and the ways in which communication shapes our relationships.

The Neuroscience of Connection

Human connection is deeply rooted in our biology. Our brains are wired to connect with others, and social interactions play a crucial role in our mental and emotional well-being. Neuroscientists have identified specific neural circuits and neurotransmitters involved in social bonding and communication.

For instance, the hormone oxytocin, often referred to as the "love hormone" or "bonding hormone," is released during positive social interactions. Oxytocin promotes feelings of trust, empathy, and connection, reinforcing social bonds. This neurochemical response highlights the importance of positive social interactions for our emotional health.

Additionally, research on mirror neurons has shown that our brains are capable of mirroring the emotions and actions of others. This neural mirroring plays a key role in empathy, allowing us to understand and resonate with the emotions of those around us. It is through this empathic connection that we build deep, meaningful relationships.

The Psychology of Communication

Psychological research provides insights into the cognitive and emotional processes that underpin effective communication. Studies on active listening, emotional intelligence, and social cognition reveal the skills and behaviors that foster successful interactions.

Active listening, for example, involves fully engaging with the speaker, paying attention to their words, tone, and body language, and responding with empathy and understanding. This skill enhances communication by creating a sense of validation and respect, encouraging open and honest dialogue.

Emotional intelligence, which encompasses self-awareness, self-regulation, empathy, and social skills, is another critical component of effective communication. High emotional intelligence enables us to navigate our own emotions and understand the emotions of others, facilitating more constructive and empathetic interactions.

Social cognition research explores how we perceive, interpret, and respond to social information. This includes understanding social cues, reading body language, and interpreting the intentions and emotions of others. By honing our social cognition skills, we can improve our ability to connect and communicate effectively in diverse social contexts.

The Sociology of Relationships

Sociological research examines the broader social and cultural factors that influence our relationships. This includes the impact of social norms, cultural values, and social structures on our communication patterns and relationship dynamics.

Social norms and cultural values shape our expectations and behaviors in interactions. Understanding these influences allows us to navigate social dynamics more effectively, adapting our communication style to fit different cultural and social contexts. This cultural competence is particularly important in an increasingly globalized world, where we interact with people from diverse backgrounds.

Social structures, such as family, work, and community networks, also play a crucial role in shaping our relationships. These structures provide the context in which our interactions take place, influencing the opportunities and challenges we face in building connections. By understanding the impact of these social structures, we can better navigate the complexities of our relationships and create more supportive and fulfilling social networks.

Integrating Science and Practice

The insights from neuroscience, psychology, and sociology provide a rich understanding of the foundations of human connection. By integrating these scientific perspectives with practical communication skills, we can enhance our ability to connect with others in meaningful and impactful ways.

In this book, we will explore a range of techniques and practices to develop these skills, from active listening and empathy to conflict resolution and cultural competence. Through a combination of scientific insights and practical exercises, you will gain the tools and knowledge needed to become a master communicator, capable of creating genuine human connections that enrich your life and the lives of those around you.

Chapter 2

Practical Conversations: The Basics of Information Exchange

Practical conversations form the backbone of our daily interactions, focusing on the clear and effective exchange of information. These conversations are fundamental to organizing our lives, completing tasks, and ensuring smooth communication in both personal and professional contexts. It focuses on identifying practical conversations, techniques for clear and effective communication, and overcoming common communication barriers.

Identifying Practical Conversations

In the realm of human interaction, practical conversations are the backbone of daily communication. These exchanges, often perceived as mundane, are vital for the seamless functioning of our personal and professional lives. They revolve around the transmission of information, ideas, and instructions, ensuring that our needs are met, tasks are accomplished, and plans are coordinated. Recognizing practical conversations and understanding their significance is the first step towards mastering the art of effective communication.

Practical conversations typically involve clear, concise exchanges that serve a specific purpose. These interactions are straightforward, focusing on the immediate and tangible aspects of our lives. Examples include discussing schedules, giving directions, planning events, and sharing updates. While they may seem routine, the importance of practical conversations cannot be overstated. They form the foundation upon which more complex and emotionally charged interactions are built.

To identify a practical conversation, one must pay attention to the context and content of the exchange. Practical conversations are goal-oriented, driven by the need to convey or obtain specific information. They often begin with direct questions or statements, such as "What time is the meeting?" or "Can you send me the report by Friday?" The clarity of purpose in these conversations is a distinguishing feature, setting them apart from more nuanced and layered interactions.

Moreover, practical conversations are characterized by their efficiency and brevity. The primary aim is to communicate the necessary information as quickly and accurately as possible, minimizing the risk of misunderstandings. In contrast to emotional or social conversations, where the focus is on building relationships and expressing feelings, practical conversations prioritize functionality and precision. By honing the ability to identify these exchanges, individuals can navigate their daily interactions with greater ease and effectiveness.

Techniques for Clear and Effective Communication

Mastering practical conversations requires a set of techniques that enhance clarity and effectiveness. These techniques are essential for ensuring that the intended message is accurately conveyed and understood. Effective communication is not only about speaking clearly but also about listening actively and responding appropriately. Here are some key strategies for improving practical communication skills:

Clarity and Brevity

The hallmark of a successful practical conversation is clarity. To achieve this, it is crucial to be direct and specific in your communication. Avoid using ambiguous language or vague expressions that can lead to misunderstandings. Instead, focus on conveying your message in a straightforward manner. For example, instead of saying, "Let's meet sometime next week," specify, "Let's meet on Tuesday at 10 AM."

Brevity is equally important. Long-winded explanations can dilute the core message and confuse the listener. Aim to be concise, providing just enough information to achieve the conversation's objective. This not only saves time but also ensures that the essential points are communicated effectively.

Active Listening

Effective communication is a two-way street. While speaking clearly is important, listening actively is equally crucial. Active listening involves paying full attention to the speaker, understanding their message, and responding thoughtfully. This means avoiding distractions, maintaining eye contact, and nodding or giving verbal acknowledgments to show that you are engaged.

Active listening also involves paraphrasing or summarizing what the speaker has said to confirm your understanding. For example, you might say, "So, you're saying that the project deadline is next Monday, correct?" This technique helps to clarify any potential misunderstandings and ensures that both parties are on the same page.

Asking Questions

Asking questions is a powerful tool for effective communication. It helps to clarify information, gather additional details, and ensure mutual understanding. Open-ended questions, such as "Can you explain more about this?" encourage the speaker to provide more comprehensive answers, while closed-ended questions, like "Is the meeting at 3 PM?" help to confirm specific details.

Questions also demonstrate your interest and engagement in the conversation, fostering a more collaborative and productive interaction. By asking the right questions, you can guide the conversation towards its intended goal and address any uncertainties that may arise.

Providing Feedback

Feedback is an essential component of effective communication. It involves giving and receiving constructive input to improve the quality of the conversation. Positive feedback, such as acknowledging a well-delivered message, reinforces good communication practices. Constructive feedback, on the other hand, addresses areas for improvement in a respectful and supportive manner.

When providing feedback, be specific and focus on the behavior or message rather than the person. For example, instead of saying, "You're not clear," you might say, "I didn't quite understand the last part of your explanation. Could you clarify it for me?" This approach fosters a positive and open communication environment.

Nonverbal Communication

Nonverbal cues, such as body language, facial expressions, and tone of voice, play a significant role in practical conversations. These cues can reinforce or contradict the spoken message, affecting how it is received and interpreted. For instance, maintaining an open posture and using a friendly tone can make your communication more approachable and effective.

Being aware of your own nonverbal signals and interpreting those of others can enhance your communication skills. Pay attention to cues such as eye contact, gestures, and vocal intonation to ensure that your message is conveyed accurately and respectfully.

Overcoming Common Communication Barriers

Despite the best intentions, practical conversations can be hindered by various communication barriers. These barriers can lead to misunderstandings, frustration, and a breakdown in communication. Identifying and addressing these obstacles is essential for fostering effective and productive interactions. Here are some common communication barriers and strategies to overcome them:

Language and Jargon

Language differences and the use of technical jargon can create significant barriers in practical conversations. When communicating with individuals from different linguistic backgrounds or fields, it is important to use clear and simple language. Avoid using industry-specific terms or acronyms that may not be understood by the listener.

If specialized terminology is necessary, take the time to explain it. For example, instead of saying, "The KPI metrics need to be optimized," you might say, "The key performance indicators (KPIs) need to be improved to measure our success more effectively." Providing context and definitions can bridge the gap and ensure mutual understanding.

Assumptions and Misconceptions

Assumptions and misconceptions can distort the message and lead to misunderstandings. It is important to avoid making assumptions about what the other person knows or intends. Instead, verify information and clarify any uncertainties.

Encourage open dialogue by asking for confirmation and feedback. For example, you might say, "I want to make sure I understand correctly. Are you suggesting that we change the project timeline?" This approach helps to clarify intentions and prevent miscommunication.

Emotional Barriers

Emotions can significantly impact practical conversations. Stress, frustration, or anger can hinder clear communication and lead to misunderstandings. It is important to manage emotions and approach conversations with a calm and composed demeanor.

If emotions are running high, it may be helpful to take a break and revisit the conversation later. This allows both parties to cool down and approach the discussion with a clearer mindset. Practicing empathy and understanding the emotional state of others can also facilitate more effective communication.

Distractions and Interruptions

Distractions and interruptions can disrupt the flow of a conversation and hinder effective communication. It is important to create an environment conducive to focused and uninterrupted dialogue. This may involve finding a quiet space, minimizing background noise, and setting aside dedicated time for the conversation.

Additionally, avoid multitasking during important conversations. Give your full attention to the speaker and the topic at hand. This demonstrates respect and ensures that the conversation remains productive and meaningful.

Cultural Differences

Cultural differences can influence communication styles, norms, and expectations. It is important to be aware of and sensitive to these differences when engaging in practical conversations. This involves understanding cultural nuances, such as appropriate greetings, gestures, and communication protocols.

When communicating with individuals from different cultural backgrounds, take the time to learn about their customs and preferences. This cultural competence can enhance mutual understanding and foster more respectful and effective interactions.

By understanding the foundations of practical conversations and mastering the techniques for clear and effective communication, individuals can navigate their daily interactions with greater ease and success. Practical conversations, though often perceived as routine, are essential for building and maintaining relationships, achieving goals, and fostering a sense of connection and trust. Through mindful communication and the ability to overcome common barriers, we can elevate our practical conversations and enhance our overall communication skills, leading to more fulfilling and meaningful interactions in all aspects of life.

Chapter 3

Emotional Conversations: Navigating Feelings and Empathy

Emotional conversations are at the heart of human connection. They allow us to express our innermost thoughts, fears, joys, and sorrows, fostering deeper understanding and intimacy in our relationships. Navigating these conversations effectively requires emotional intelligence, empathy, and the ability to listen and respond with sensitivity. This further explores the depths of emotional conversations, how to build emotional intelligence, and tools for empathetic listening and response.

Understanding Emotional Depth in Conversations

Emotional conversations are the heartbeats of our relationships, infusing them with depth and meaning. They go beyond the surface level of exchanging information, delving into the realm of feelings, vulnerabilities, and personal experiences. These conversations are crucial because they foster genuine connections, build trust, and allow us to understand and be understood on a profound level.

Understanding the emotional depth in conversations requires us to recognize and value the importance of emotions in our interactions. Emotions are powerful communicators; they reveal our innermost thoughts and desires, and they influence our actions and decisions. When we engage in emotional conversations, we open ourselves up to share our true selves with others, creating a space for authenticity and intimacy.

Consider the difference between a casual conversation about the weather and a heartfelt discussion about a significant life event, such as losing a loved one or achieving a long-desired goal. The latter is rich with emotional content, allowing the individuals involved to connect on a deeper level. These conversations require a different approach than practical exchanges; they demand sensitivity, empathy, and a willingness to be vulnerable.

Emotional conversations often revolve around themes such as love, fear, joy, and sorrow. They can be challenging because they touch on sensitive areas of our lives, but they are also incredibly rewarding. By understanding the emotional depth in these conversations, we can navigate them more effectively, fostering stronger and more meaningful relationships.

Building Emotional Intelligence

Emotional intelligence (EI) is the cornerstone of navigating emotional conversations successfully. It refers to the ability to recognize, understand, and manage our own emotions, as well as the emotions of others. High emotional intelligence allows us to communicate more effectively, build deeper connections, and handle conflicts with grace.

Self-Awareness

The first step in building emotional intelligence is self-awareness. This involves recognizing our own emotions and understanding how they affect our thoughts and behavior. Self-awareness allows us to stay in tune with our feelings, making it easier to express them appropriately in conversations.

For example, imagine you are feeling stressed about a work deadline. Recognizing this stress and its impact on your mood can help you communicate your needs more effectively to your team. You might say, "I'm feeling overwhelmed with this project and could use some help to meet the deadline." This honest expression of your emotions can foster understanding and collaboration.

Self-Regulation

Self-regulation is the ability to manage our emotions, especially in challenging situations. It involves controlling impulsive reactions, staying calm under pressure, and responding thoughtfully rather than reactively. This skill is crucial in emotional conversations, where heightened emotions can easily lead to misunderstandings or conflicts.

Consider a situation where you receive critical feedback from a colleague. Instead of reacting defensively, self-regulation allows you to take a moment to process your emotions and respond constructively. You might say, "Thank you for your feedback. I'll take it into consideration and work on improving." This measured response shows maturity and a willingness to grow.

Empathy

Empathy is the ability to understand and share the feelings of others. It is a vital component of emotional intelligence, enabling us to connect with others on a deep emotional level. Empathy involves actively listening to others, recognizing their emotions, and responding with compassion and understanding.

For instance, if a friend shares that they are going through a difficult breakup, empathy allows you to offer genuine support. Instead of offering platitudes, you might say, "I'm so sorry to hear that. I can't imagine how tough this must be for you. I'm here if you need to talk." This empathetic response acknowledges their pain and offers a comforting presence.

Social Skills

Strong social skills are essential for navigating emotional conversations and building meaningful relationships. These skills include effective communication, conflict resolution, and the ability to build rapport with others. Social skills help us navigate the complexities of interpersonal interactions and foster positive connections.

Effective communication involves not only expressing our own emotions but also understanding and validating the emotions of others. Conflict resolution skills allow us to address disagreements constructively, finding solutions that satisfy all parties involved. Building rapport involves creating a sense of trust and connection through genuine interest and respect.

By developing emotional intelligence, we can navigate emotional conversations with greater ease and effectiveness. These skills enhance our ability to connect with others, build trust, and foster meaningful relationships.

Tools for Empathetic Listening and Response

Empathetic listening and response are essential tools for navigating emotional conversations. They involve fully engaging with the speaker, understanding their emotions, and responding in a way that validates their feelings and fosters connection. Here are some practical tools for enhancing empathetic listening and response:

Active Listening

Active listening is the foundation of empathetic communication. It involves giving your full attention to the speaker, listening without interrupting, and responding thoughtfully. Active listening demonstrates respect and genuine interest in the speaker's perspective.

To practice active listening, focus on the speaker's words, tone, and body language. Avoid distractions and maintain eye contact to show that you are fully engaged. Use verbal cues, such as "I understand" or "Tell me more," to encourage the speaker to share their thoughts and feelings.

Reflective Listening

Reflective listening involves paraphrasing or summarizing what the speaker has said to confirm your understanding and show that you are paying attention.

This technique helps to clarify the speaker's message and demonstrates empathy.

For example, if a friend says, "I'm feeling really stressed about my exams," you might respond, "It sounds like you're under a lot of pressure with your exams. That must be really tough." This reflective response shows that you are listening and validates their feelings.

Open-Ended Questions

Open-ended questions encourage the speaker to elaborate on their thoughts and feelings, creating a deeper and more meaningful conversation. These questions cannot be answered with a simple "yes" or "no," prompting the speaker to share more detailed information.

For instance, instead of asking, "Are you okay?" you might ask, "How are you feeling about everything that's going on?" This open-ended question invites the speaker to express their emotions more fully, fostering a deeper connection.

Validation and Support

Validation involves acknowledging and accepting the speaker's emotions, even if you do not necessarily agree with their perspective. This technique helps to create a safe and supportive environment for emotional expression.

To validate the speaker's emotions, use phrases such as "I understand why you feel that way" or "It's okay to feel upset about this." Offering support, such as "I'm here for you" or "Let me know how I can help," further reinforces your empathy and commitment to the relationship.

Nonverbal Communication

Nonverbal cues, such as body language, facial expressions, and tone of voice, play a significant role in empathetic listening and response. These cues can convey empathy, understanding, and support, even without words.

Maintain an open and relaxed posture, make appropriate eye contact, and use facial expressions that reflect empathy and concern. A gentle tone of voice can also communicate compassion and understanding, enhancing the emotional depth of the conversation.

Avoiding Judgment

Empathetic listening requires a nonjudgmental attitude. It is important to approach emotional conversations with an open mind, avoiding criticism or judgment of the speaker's feelings and experiences.

Instead of offering unsolicited advice or making judgments, focus on understanding the speaker's perspective. Use phrases such as "I can see how you would feel that way" or "That sounds really challenging." This nonjudgmental approach fosters a safe space for emotional expression and builds trust in the relationship.

Patience and Presence

Patience and presence are essential qualities for empathetic listening. Emotional conversations can be difficult and may require time for the speaker to fully express their feelings. Being patient and fully present demonstrates your commitment to understanding and supporting the speaker.

Avoid rushing the conversation or interrupting the speaker. Allow them to take their time and express themselves at their own pace. Your patience and presence create a supportive environment where the speaker feels heard and valued.

By integrating these tools into our communication practices, we can navigate emotional conversations with greater empathy and effectiveness. These techniques enhance our ability to listen, understand, and respond to the emotions of others, fostering deeper and more meaningful connections.

To illustrate the power of empathetic communication, consider the following scenarios:

Supporting a Friend in Crisis

Sarah receives a phone call from her friend Emily, who is visibly upset. Emily shares that she has just lost her job and is feeling overwhelmed and scared about the future. Sarah practices active listening by giving her full attention to Emily, avoiding distractions, and using verbal cues to show she is engaged.

Sarah uses reflective listening by summarizing Emily's concerns: "It sounds like losing your job has been a huge shock, and you're worried about what comes next." She then asks open-ended questions to encourage Emily to share more: "How are you feeling about this? What's been the hardest part for you?"

Throughout the conversation, Sarah validates Emily's emotions: "It's completely understandable to feel scared and overwhelmed right now. This is a really tough situation." She offers support: "I'm here for you, and we'll figure this out together. Let me know how I can help."

Sarah's empathetic listening and response create a safe and supportive environment for Emily to express her feelings, fostering a deeper connection and providing comfort during a difficult time.

Resolving a Conflict with a Partner

John and his partner, Lisa, have been arguing about their differing parenting styles. John feels frustrated because he believes Lisa is too lenient, while Lisa feels hurt because she thinks John is too strict. They decide to have an emotional conversation to address their concerns.

John practices self-awareness by recognizing his frustration and its impact on his communication. He approaches the conversation with a calm

Chapter 4

Social Conversations: The Role of Social Context

Social conversations are the threads that weave the fabric of our social lives. They encompass a wide range of interactions, from casual small talk to deep discussions about societal issues. These conversations are influenced by the social context in which they occur, including cultural norms, group dynamics, and individual roles within a social setting. It explores the role of social context in conversations, strategies for social awareness and adaptability, and how to create inclusive and positive social interactions.

Recognizing Social Dynamics in Conversations

Social conversations are intricate dances of norms, roles, and expectations that shape our interactions within various contexts. Unlike practical conversations that focus on information exchange or emotional conversations that delve into personal feelings, social conversations revolve around establishing and maintaining relationships, navigating social hierarchies, and adhering to cultural norms.

At the heart of social dynamics in conversations lies the understanding that our interactions are influenced by a myriad of factors, including societal expectations, cultural backgrounds, and individual personalities. These dynamics dictate how we present ourselves, interpret others' behavior, and negotiate our place within social settings.

For example, consider a networking event where professionals gather to establish connections. The conversations that unfold are not merely exchanges of business cards or resumes; they are strategic interactions aimed at building rapport, demonstrating expertise, and forging alliances. Understanding the social dynamics at play allows individuals to navigate these situations with finesse, making a positive impression and cultivating valuable relationships.

Moreover, social conversations encompass a spectrum of interactions, from casual chit-chat at social gatherings to formal discussions in professional settings. Each context brings its own set of expectations and norms, requiring individuals to adapt their communication style accordingly. By recognizing these social dynamics, we can engage more effectively with others, foster mutual understanding, and cultivate meaningful connections.

Strategies for Social Awareness and Adaptability

Navigating social conversations with finesse requires both awareness of social cues and adaptability in our communication approach. Social awareness involves perceiving and understanding the emotions, intentions, and dynamics of others, while adaptability allows us to adjust our behavior to fit different social contexts and personalities.

Observational Skills

Observational skills are essential for social awareness. Pay attention to nonverbal cues such as body language, facial expressions, and tone of voice to gauge the emotional state and reactions of others. For example, crossed arms and a furrowed brow may indicate discomfort or disagreement, while a smile and relaxed posture suggest openness and agreement.

By observing these cues, you can tailor your communication style and approach to better align with the social dynamics of the conversation. This enhances your ability to connect with others and build rapport effectively.

Contextual Understanding

Understanding the social context in which conversations occur is key to navigating them successfully. Consider factors such as the setting, participants' roles and relationships, and the purpose of the interaction. For instance, a team meeting may require a more formal and structured communication style compared to a brainstorming session among colleagues.

Adapt your language, tone, and behavior to match the expectations of the social context. This demonstrates respect for cultural norms and enhances your ability to communicate persuasively and influentially.

Flexibility in Communication

Flexibility in communication involves adjusting your approach based on the needs and preferences of others. This may include modulating your tone of voice, using appropriate language, and adapting your conversational style to accommodate different personalities and communication styles.

For example, when engaging with an introverted colleague, you may adopt a more reflective and attentive listening approach to encourage their participation.

Conversely, when interacting with a charismatic leader, you may mirror their energy and enthusiasm to establish rapport and alignment.

Empathetic Engagement

Empathetic engagement involves demonstrating empathy and understanding towards others' perspectives and emotions. This fosters a supportive and inclusive environment where individuals feel valued and respected. Practice active listening, validate others' viewpoints, and offer constructive feedback to promote mutual understanding and collaboration.

For instance, if a team member expresses concerns about a project deadline, demonstrate empathy by acknowledging their challenges and offering practical solutions or support. This empathetic approach strengthens relationships and encourages open communication within teams and organizations.

Cultural Sensitivity

Cultural sensitivity is essential in navigating diverse social contexts and fostering inclusive interactions. Respect cultural differences in communication styles, customs, and values to avoid misunderstandings and promote harmony. Learn about the cultural backgrounds of others and adapt your behavior accordingly to demonstrate respect and appreciation.

For example, when interacting with international colleagues, be mindful of differences in greeting etiquette, personal space norms, and hierarchical structures. Adjust your communication style to align with cultural preferences and build trust and rapport across cultural boundaries.

Creating Inclusive and Positive Social Interactions

Creating inclusive and positive social interactions requires intentional effort and a commitment to fostering mutual respect and understanding. By embracing diversity, celebrating differences, and promoting inclusivity, we can create environments where everyone feels valued and empowered to contribute.

Respect and Open-Mindedness

Respect for others' perspectives, experiences, and identities is fundamental to creating inclusive social interactions. Approach conversations with an open mind, listen actively, and refrain from making assumptions or judgments based on stereotypes or biases. Cultivate a culture of respect where diverse viewpoints are welcomed and valued.

For example, in a team meeting discussing a new project, encourage all members to share their ideas and perspectives, regardless of hierarchy or background. Create a safe space where individuals feel comfortable expressing themselves and contributing to collaborative decision-making.

Encouraging Participation

Encouraging participation involves promoting equal opportunities for all individuals to contribute and be heard in social conversations. Actively seek input from quieter or less assertive participants, and ensure that everyone has the opportunity to share their thoughts and ideas.

For instance, during a group discussion, invite quieter members to speak by asking direct questions or providing opportunities for them to share their perspectives. Acknowledge and validate their contributions to foster a sense of belonging and inclusivity within the group.

Building Bridges Across Differences

Building bridges across differences involves fostering connections and understanding among individuals from diverse backgrounds. Encourage dialogue and collaboration across cultural, generational, and organizational boundaries to promote empathy, mutual respect, and collaboration.

For example, organize cross-cultural exchanges or diversity training workshops to facilitate meaningful interactions and promote cultural awareness within teams and organizations. By building bridges across differences, we can strengthen relationships, foster innovation, and create inclusive environments where everyone can thrive.

Conflict Resolution and Mediation

Conflict resolution and mediation are essential skills for addressing disagreements and promoting positive social interactions. Encourage open communication, listen to all perspectives, and seek mutually agreeable solutions that respect the interests and needs of all parties involved.

For example, if tensions arise during a team meeting or social gathering, facilitate a constructive dialogue where individuals can express their concerns and work together to find common ground. Use active listening and empathy to de-escalate conflicts and promote understanding and reconciliation.

Promoting Positive Communication Norms

Promoting positive communication norms involves establishing guidelines and practices that support respectful, constructive, and inclusive interactions. Encourage transparency, honesty, and empathy in communication, and discourage behaviors that undermine trust or create barriers to collaboration.

For instance, establish ground rules for meetings or group discussions that promote active listening, respect for diverse viewpoints, and constructive feedback. Model positive communication behaviors and hold individuals accountable for upholding these norms to create a culture of trust and mutual respect.

By recognizing social dynamics in conversations, employing strategies for social awareness and adaptability, and creating inclusive and positive social interactions, we can enhance our ability to navigate complex social landscapes with confidence and authenticity. Social conversations offer opportunities for building meaningful connections, fostering collaboration, and promoting mutual understanding across diverse contexts. As we continue to explore the role of social context in communication, we deepen our appreciation for the richness and complexity of human interactions, paving the way for more inclusive and harmonious relationships in our personal and professional lives.

Chapter 5

The Art of Recognizing and Matching Conversations

Effective communication is not just about exchanging words; it's about understanding the layers beneath each conversation and navigating them with finesse. The ability to recognize and match the tone and nature of a conversation is a crucial skill in effective communication. It allows you to connect with others more meaningfully and ensures that your interactions are productive and respectful. It focuses on identifying the dominant layer in any conversation, techniques for matching conversation layers, and provides case studies that illustrate successful connection through this approach.

Identifying the Dominant Layer in Any Conversation

Every conversation unfolds across multiple layers: practical, emotional, and social. The dominant layer determines the primary focus and tone of the interaction, shaping how information is exchanged and relationships are formed.

Practical Conversations

Practical conversations center around exchanging information, facts, and details. They are straightforward and goal-oriented, focusing on tasks, plans, or logistics. For example, discussing project deadlines, scheduling appointments, or sharing factual updates are typical instances of practical conversations.

Identifying practical conversations involves recognizing cues such as direct questions, factual statements, or discussions about specific actions or outcomes. These conversations are essential for achieving objectives, making decisions, and coordinating activities effectively.

Emotional Conversations

Emotional conversations revolve around feelings, experiences, and personal perspectives. They delve into emotions such as joy, sadness, anger, or fear, allowing individuals to express their inner thoughts and vulnerabilities. For instance, sharing personal stories, discussing challenges, or expressing empathy are common themes in emotional conversations.

Recognizing emotional conversations requires sensitivity to nonverbal cues, tone of voice, and the intensity of emotions expressed. These conversations create opportunities for bonding, building trust, and deepening relationships based on shared experiences and mutual understanding.

Social Conversations

Social conversations focus on establishing rapport, navigating social norms, and maintaining relationships. They involve topics such as shared interests, cultural references, or social events, fostering camaraderie and a sense of belonging within groups. For example, chatting about hobbies, discussing current events, or sharing anecdotes about mutual acquaintances are typical social interactions.

Identifying social conversations involves observing conversational cues such as small talk, humor, gestures of politeness, or references to shared experiences. These conversations play a crucial role in building social connections, fostering goodwill, and strengthening community bonds.

Techniques for Matching Conversation Layers

Matching conversation layers involves aligning your communication style, tone, and content with the dominant layer of the conversation. This skill enhances rapport, facilitates understanding, and promotes meaningful engagement with others.

Active Listening and Observation

Active listening is fundamental to matching conversation layers effectively. Pay attention to verbal cues, nonverbal signals, and the overall context of the conversation to discern its dominant layer. Reflect on the emotions, topics, and social dynamics at play to guide your responses and interactions accordingly.

For example, if a colleague shares their excitement about a recent achievement (emotional layer), respond empathetically by acknowledging their accomplishment and sharing in their joy. Avoid shifting the focus to practical details or unrelated topics, as this may disrupt the emotional connection established.

Adaptability in Communication Style

Adaptability allows you to adjust your communication style to resonate with the dominant layer of the conversation. Tailor your language, tone of voice, and level of formality to match the preferences and expectations of your conversation partner(s). This demonstrates respect, enhances clarity, and promotes effective communication.

For instance, in a practical conversation focused on project planning, maintain a concise and task-oriented communication style to facilitate clarity and efficiency. Conversely, in an emotional conversation where a friend expresses concern about a personal challenge, adopt a supportive and compassionate tone to convey empathy and understanding.

Responding with Sensitivity and Empathy

Responding with sensitivity and empathy involves acknowledging and validating the emotions, perspectives, and experiences shared within the conversation. Validate feelings, demonstrate understanding, and offer support or encouragement as appropriate. This fosters trust, strengthens relationships, and promotes a supportive environment for open communication.

For example, if a family member expresses sadness over a recent loss (emotional layer), respond with empathy by offering condolences and providing a listening ear. Avoid minimizing their feelings or offering unsolicited advice, as this may undermine their emotional experience and disrupt the connection established.

Case Studies: Successful Connection through Layer Matching

Case studies provide real-world examples of successful connection achieved through effective recognition and matching of conversation layers. These stories illustrate how individuals leverage their understanding of practical, emotional, and social dynamics to foster meaningful interactions and build lasting relationships.

Networking Event

At a professional networking event, Alex encounters a potential client, Sarah. Initially, their conversation revolves around practical topics such as industry trends and business challenges (practical layer). Recognizing Sarah's enthusiasm for innovation, Alex shifts the conversation to emotional themes by sharing personal success stories and discussing their mutual passion for creativity and problem-solving.

By matching the emotional layer of the conversation, Alex establishes a deeper connection with Sarah, demonstrating shared values and aspirations. This emotional resonance strengthens their professional rapport and lays the foundation for future collaboration and partnership.

Family Gathering

During a family gathering, Emma notices her cousin, Jake, looking visibly upset (emotional layer). Sensing his discomfort, Emma approaches Jake with empathy and asks if he would like to talk privately. In a quiet corner, Jake opens up about his recent struggles at work and feelings of uncertainty about his career path.

Emma listens actively, offering emotional support and reassurance without judgment. She validates Jake's feelings and shares her own experiences of overcoming challenges, creating a safe space for him to express himself openly. Through empathetic listening and response, Emma strengthens her bond with Jake and reinforces their family connection based on trust and understanding.

Recognizing and matching conversation layers is a transformative skill that enhances our ability to connect authentically, communicate effectively, and build meaningful relationships. By understanding the dynamics of practical, emotional, and social conversations, we navigate interpersonal interactions with insight and sensitivity, fostering mutual understanding and fostering harmonious relationships in our personal and professional lives. As we continue to refine our approach to conversation layer matching, we empower ourselves to cultivate richer connections, nurture empathy, and create positive impacts within our communities and beyond.

Chapter 6

Navigating Complex Emotions and Beliefs

Emotions and beliefs are the bedrock of human experience, shaping our interactions, decisions, and relationships. We will embark on a journey through the labyrinth of complex emotions and beliefs, exploring how to navigate these intricate landscapes with empathy, clarity, and mutual respect.

Understanding Emotional Triggers and Responses

Emotional triggers are catalysts that ignite intense feelings within us, often rooted in past experiences, values, or personal insecurities. Understanding our emotional triggers allows us to recognize the source of our reactions and respond thoughtfully rather than reactively.

Identification of Emotional Triggers

Identifying emotional triggers begins with self-awareness and introspection. Reflect on moments when you have experienced heightened emotions such as anger, fear, sadness, or joy. Consider the circumstances, individuals involved, and underlying beliefs or expectations that contributed to your emotional response.

For example, criticism from a colleague may trigger feelings of defensiveness or inadequacy, stemming from a fear of failure or desire for approval. By identifying these triggers, we gain insight into our emotional landscape and empower ourselves to manage our responses more effectively.

Emotional Regulation Techniques

Emotional regulation techniques are strategies that help us manage and navigate intense emotions constructively. These techniques promote self-control, resilience, and emotional well-being, enhancing our ability to engage in meaningful conversations and maintain positive relationships.

Practice mindfulness and deep breathing exercises to center yourself during moments of stress or agitation. Use cognitive reframing to challenge negative thoughts and replace them with more balanced perspectives. Engage in physical activities such as exercise or creative expression to release pent-up emotions and promote relaxation.

By cultivating emotional regulation skills, we develop greater emotional intelligence and adaptive coping mechanisms, enabling us to navigate complex emotions with composure and clarity.

Negotiating Differing Beliefs with Respect

Beliefs shape our worldview, influencing how we perceive ourselves, others, and the world around us. When engaging in conversations with individuals who hold differing beliefs, approaching these interactions with respect, openness, and curiosity is essential to fostering mutual understanding and constructive dialogue.

Active Listening and Validation

Active listening is foundational to negotiating differing beliefs with respect. Listen attentively to others' viewpoints without interrupting or immediately rebutting. Seek to understand their beliefs, values, and experiences that inform their perspective.

Validate their feelings and perspectives, acknowledging the validity of their beliefs within their own lived experiences. Avoid dismissing or invalidating their beliefs, as this can lead to defensiveness and hinder productive dialogue.

Empathetic Perspective-Taking

Empathetic perspective-taking involves stepping into the shoes of others to understand their beliefs from their perspective. Consider the influences, experiences, and cultural backgrounds that shape their worldview. Cultivate empathy by imagining how you would feel and think if you held similar beliefs.

For example, if discussing political ideologies with a friend who holds opposing views, practice empathetic perspective-taking by exploring the values and societal concerns underlying their beliefs. This approach fosters empathy, promotes mutual respect, and bridges the gap between differing perspectives.

Constructive Dialogue and Compromise

Constructive dialogue entails exchanging ideas, sharing perspectives, and exploring common ground. Focus on areas of agreement or shared goals to build rapport and facilitate collaboration. Seek compromises or solutions that honor both parties' beliefs and values while promoting mutual respect and understanding.

For instance, in a team setting where members have differing opinions on project strategies, encourage open dialogue and brainstorming to find creative solutions that integrate diverse perspectives. Embrace diversity of thought as a strength that enriches decision-making and promotes innovation.

Building Bridges in Difficult Conversations

Difficult conversations often arise when discussing sensitive topics or navigating conflicting viewpoints. Building bridges in these conversations requires courage, empathy, and a commitment to fostering mutual respect and understanding.

Establishing a Safe and Respectful Environment

Create a safe and respectful environment where all participants feel valued and heard. Set ground rules for communication, such as active listening, speaking respectfully, and refraining from personal attacks. Foster an atmosphere of openness and trust that encourages honest dialogue and vulnerability.

For example, in a family discussion about healthcare decisions for an elderly parent, establish a safe space where each family member can express their concerns and preferences without judgment. Encourage empathy and mutual support to navigate emotional complexities with compassion and understanding.

Managing Emotional Intensity

Emotional intensity can escalate during difficult conversations, potentially derailing constructive dialogue. Practice emotional regulation techniques to manage your own emotions and diffuse tension within the conversation. Use calming strategies such as taking deep breaths, pausing to reflect, or suggesting a temporary break if emotions become overwhelming.

For instance, if discussing sensitive topics such as religious beliefs with friends of different faiths, acknowledge the emotional significance of the conversation and approach it with sensitivity and respect. Create opportunities for reflection and mutual understanding to bridge differences and strengthen relationships.

Seeking Common Ground and Shared Goals

Seeking common ground and shared goals facilitates consensus-building and collaboration in difficult conversations. Identify areas of agreement or mutual interests that can serve as a foundation for finding solutions or compromises that honor diverse perspectives.

For example, in a community meeting discussing environmental sustainability, focus on shared values such as preserving natural resources and promoting eco-friendly practices. Collaborate on actionable initiatives that align with these shared goals, fostering unity and collective action.

Navigating complex emotions and beliefs is a transformative journey that requires empathy, self-awareness, and a commitment to mutual respect. By understanding emotional triggers and responses, negotiating differing beliefs with respect, and building bridges in difficult conversations, we cultivate meaningful connections, promote understanding, and foster harmony within our interpersonal relationships and communities. As we continue to navigate the intricate landscapes of human emotions and beliefs, we deepen our capacity for empathy, strengthen our communication skills, and contribute to a more compassionate and inclusive society.

Chapter 7

The Influence of Experiences and Values

Our personal histories and core values serve as compasses guiding our interactions, shaping how we communicate, connect, and relate to others. We will explore the profound influence of experiences and values on communication, highlighting their role in fostering deeper connections, aligning beliefs, and honoring the diversity of perspectives that enrich our interactions.

How Personal Histories Shape Communication

Personal histories are tapestries woven from our unique life experiences, memories, and formative moments. These narratives not only define who we are but also influence how we perceive the world and engage in interpersonal relationships.

Narrative Identity

Narrative identity refers to the stories we tell ourselves about our past, present, and future selves. These narratives shape our sense of identity, values, and beliefs, providing a framework through which we interpret and communicate our experiences to others.

For example, someone who has overcome adversity may view challenges as opportunities for growth and resilience, while another person with a privileged upbringing may emphasize the importance of social responsibility and empathy. Understanding these narrative identities allows us to appreciate the diversity of perspectives and experiences that shape communication dynamics.

Cultural and Interpersonal Context

Cultural and interpersonal contexts play pivotal roles in shaping communication styles and norms. Cultural values, traditions, and societal norms influence how individuals express themselves, perceive authority, and navigate social interactions.

For instance, in cultures that prioritize collective harmony and indirect communication, individuals may use implicit cues and nonverbal gestures to convey messages. In contrast, cultures that value individualism and direct communication may emphasize clarity, assertiveness, and transparency in interpersonal exchanges.

Aligning Values for Deeper Connection

Values serve as guiding principles that reflect our beliefs, priorities, and ethical standards. Aligning values with others fosters deeper connections, mutual understanding, and shared goals within relationships and communities.

Identifying Core Values

Identifying core values involves reflecting on what matters most to us, both personally and professionally. Core values encompass principles such as integrity, compassion, respect, and accountability, which shape our decisions, behaviors, and interactions with others.

For example, someone who values honesty and transparency may prioritize open communication and authenticity in their relationships, fostering trust and mutual respect. By aligning values with others, we create a foundation for meaningful connections based on shared principles and ethical standards.

Promoting Authenticity and Congruence

Authenticity involves aligning our actions, beliefs, and values with our true selves. It requires self-awareness, introspection, and a commitment to living in accordance with our core principles. Authentic communication promotes transparency, vulnerability, and genuine connection with others.

For instance, in professional settings, leaders who demonstrate authenticity and congruence between their words and actions inspire trust and loyalty among their teams. By modeling authenticity, they create an environment where individuals feel valued, empowered, and motivated to contribute their best.

Honoring Diversity in Perspectives

Diversity encompasses a range of perspectives, experiences, and identities that enrich our understanding of the world and broaden our collective perspectives. Honoring diversity in perspectives involves embracing differences, respecting individual viewpoints, and valuing cultural pluralism within global communities.

Cultivating Empathy and Cultural Competence

Cultivating empathy involves understanding and appreciating the perspectives, feelings, and experiences of others. Empathetic communication fosters inclusivity, promotes mutual respect, and bridges cultural divides by acknowledging and validating diverse viewpoints.

For example, in cross-cultural interactions, demonstrate curiosity and openness to learn about different customs, traditions, and societal norms. Seek common ground while celebrating cultural diversity to promote understanding and foster harmonious relationships.

Encouraging Dialogue and Collaboration

Encouraging dialogue and collaboration across diverse perspectives promotes innovation, creativity, and informed decision-making. Create opportunities for individuals from varied backgrounds to share their insights, challenge assumptions, and contribute to collective problem-solving.

For instance, in organizational settings, establish forums or workshops that facilitate open dialogue and brainstorming among employees from diverse departments or cultural backgrounds. Embrace diverse perspectives as catalysts for growth, innovation, and inclusive leadership.

The influence of experiences and values on communication is profound, shaping our identities, relationships, and interactions within diverse social contexts. By understanding how personal histories shape communication dynamics, aligning values for deeper connection, and honoring diversity in perspectives, we cultivate empathy, foster mutual respect, and promote inclusivity within our communities and beyond.

Chapter 8

Developing Advanced Communication Skills

Effective communication transcends mere words; it encompasses a nuanced interplay of non-verbal cues, persuasive techniques, and conflict resolution strategies. In this chapter, we delve into the art of developing advanced communication skills, exploring how mastering non-verbal communication, refining persuasion tactics, and employing conflict resolution techniques can foster clarity, influence, and harmony in interpersonal interactions and professional endeavors.

The Role of Non-Verbal Communication

Non-verbal communication constitutes a significant component of our daily interactions, conveying subtle messages through gestures, facial expressions, body language, and vocal tone. Understanding and harnessing the power of non-verbal cues enhances communication effectiveness, facilitates emotional connection, and reinforces verbal messages.

Types of Non-Verbal Communication

Non-verbal communication encompasses various forms, each playing a distinct role in conveying emotions, intentions, and attitudes. Facial expressions, such as smiles, frowns, or raised eyebrows, communicate emotional states and reactions. Gestures, including hand movements, nods, or posture adjustments, emphasize points, regulate conversation flow, and express engagement.

Vocal cues, such as tone of voice, pitch, and rhythm, convey emotions and attitudes, influencing how messages are perceived. For instance, a calm and soothing tone can reassure during moments of distress, while a confident and assertive voice may convey authority and conviction.

Enhancing Non-Verbal Awareness

Enhancing non-verbal awareness involves mindfulness and observation of both our own non-verbal cues and those of others. Pay attention to facial expressions, gestures, and vocal nuances to interpret underlying emotions and intentions accurately. Practice mirroring and matching non-verbal cues to establish rapport and build connection with conversation partners.

For example, in a professional setting, maintain attentive eye contact, nod affirmatively, and adopt an open posture to convey attentiveness and interest during meetings or presentations. These non-verbal behaviors reinforce active listening and encourage collaborative communication among team members.

Mastering the Art of Persuasion and Influence

Persuasion is the art of influencing others' attitudes, beliefs, and behaviors through effective communication and compelling arguments. Mastering persuasion requires strategic communication tactics, empathy, and a deep understanding of audience preferences and motivations.

Principles of Persuasion

The principles of persuasion, as outlined by psychologist Robert Cialdini, include reciprocity, scarcity, authority, consistency, liking, and consensus. These principles leverage psychological triggers to influence decision-making and shape perceptions effectively.

Apply reciprocity by offering value or assistance to others, fostering goodwill and reciprocity in return. Create a sense of scarcity by highlighting unique benefits or limited-time offers, motivating action and decision-making. Establish authority through expertise, credentials, or endorsements, enhancing credibility and trustworthiness.

Tailoring Messages to Audience Needs

Tailoring messages to audience needs involves understanding their preferences, interests, and priorities to craft persuasive arguments that resonate with their values and motivations. Conduct audience analysis to identify key concerns, objections, and aspirations, adapting communication strategies accordingly.

For instance, when persuading stakeholders to support a new initiative, emphasize how the project aligns with organizational goals, addresses current challenges, and delivers measurable benefits. Tailor messages to highlight specific outcomes and advantages that appeal to diverse stakeholder interests and perspectives.

Techniques for Conflict Resolution and Mediation

Conflict is an inevitable aspect of human interactions, stemming from differing viewpoints, priorities, and interests. Effective conflict resolution and mediation techniques promote mutual understanding, facilitate collaborative problem-solving, and preserve relationships amidst disagreement and tension.

Active Listening and Empathetic Understanding

Active listening is essential in conflict resolution, allowing individuals to fully comprehend others' perspectives, concerns, and underlying emotions. Listen attentively without interrupting, clarify points of contention, and validate feelings to demonstrate empathy and promote constructive dialogue.

Empathetic understanding involves stepping into the shoes of others to grasp their motivations, values, and aspirations. Acknowledge the validity of their viewpoints and emotions, even if you disagree, to foster trust and create a supportive environment for conflict resolution.

Collaborative Problem-Solving

Collaborative problem-solving encourages individuals to work together towards mutually acceptable solutions that address underlying issues and meet shared goals. Identify common interests, brainstorm alternative solutions, and negotiate compromises that accommodate diverse perspectives and interests.

For example, in a team experiencing conflicts over project priorities, facilitate a collaborative discussion to clarify goals, allocate resources, and establish clear timelines. Encourage open dialogue, active participation, and consensus-building to foster team cohesion and collective ownership of outcomes.

Mediation and Facilitation Techniques

Mediation involves a neutral third party facilitating communication and negotiation between conflicting parties to reach a mutually satisfactory resolution. Apply mediation techniques such as reframing issues, exploring underlying interests, and generating win-win solutions that promote reconciliation and restore harmony.

For instance, in organizational settings, trained mediators may assist employees in resolving interpersonal conflicts, navigating workplace disputes, and promoting a positive work environment. Facilitate constructive dialogue, manage emotions, and guide participants towards collaborative problem-solving to achieve lasting resolutions and strengthen interpersonal relationships.

Developing advanced communication skills is a transformative journey that empowers individuals to navigate complex interpersonal dynamics, influence outcomes, and foster harmonious relationships. By mastering non-verbal communication, refining persuasion tactics, and employing effective conflict resolution techniques, we enhance our ability to connect authentically, inspire change, and promote mutual understanding in diverse personal and professional contexts. As we continue to refine our communication skills, we contribute to a more empathetic, collaborative, and inclusive society where meaningful dialogue and constructive engagement prevail.

Chapter 9

Building Trust through Authentic Communication

Trust is the bedrock of all meaningful relationships, whether personal or professional. Authentic communication is the cornerstone of building this trust. When we communicate authentically, we express our true selves—our thoughts, feelings, and intentions—in a way that is transparent, honest, and respectful. This chapter explores the importance of authenticity in conversations, strategies for building and maintaining trust, and methods for repairing trust when it's broken.

The Importance of Authenticity in Conversations

Authenticity in communication embodies sincerity, transparency, and congruence between words, actions, and beliefs. It reflects a genuine expression of one's true self, fostering trust and credibility in interpersonal interactions. Authenticity cultivates an atmosphere of openness, vulnerability, and mutual understanding, laying the groundwork for meaningful connections and collaborative relationships.

Genuine Self-Expression

Authenticity begins with self-awareness and self-acceptance, allowing individuals to communicate their thoughts, feelings, and values honestly and openly. Authentic self-expression builds rapport, as others perceive sincerity and integrity in their interactions.

For example, in personal relationships, sharing vulnerabilities or admitting mistakes demonstrates authenticity and fosters empathy and emotional connection. Authentic communication promotes trust and deepens intimacy, creating a supportive environment where individuals feel valued and understood.

Building Trust and Credibility

Authenticity enhances trust and credibility by aligning words with actions and demonstrating consistency in behavior. When individuals communicate authentically, they establish a reputation for reliability, honesty, and integrity, reinforcing trustworthiness in their relationships.

In professional settings, leaders who exhibit authenticity inspire loyalty and commitment among team members. By communicating openly, acknowledging challenges, and celebrating successes authentically, they cultivate a culture of transparency and accountability that fosters trust and collaboration.

Strategies for Building and Maintaining Trust

Building and maintaining trust requires intentional efforts to foster transparency, reliability, and mutual respect in communication. Employing strategies that promote authenticity and demonstrate integrity enhances trustworthiness and strengthens interpersonal connections.

Open and Transparent Communication

Open and transparent communication involves sharing information, insights, and intentions openly with others. Communicate honestly about goals, expectations, and challenges to foster clarity and minimize misunderstandings.

For instance, in organizational settings, leaders who practice transparency in decision-making and communicate openly about strategic initiatives build trust among employees. Transparency promotes accountability and empowers individuals to make informed decisions, fostering a culture of trust and collaboration.

Active Listening and Empathetic Understanding

Active listening is essential to building trust, as it demonstrates respect and validates others' perspectives and emotions. Listen attentively, ask clarifying questions, and acknowledge feelings to foster empathy and deepen understanding.

Empathetic understanding involves stepping into others' shoes to grasp their experiences, values, and motivations. Show genuine interest in their concerns, validate their feelings, and demonstrate empathy to build rapport and strengthen interpersonal connections.

Consistency and Reliability

Consistency and reliability are pillars of trustworthiness, as they demonstrate predictability and dependability in behavior and actions. Honor commitments, follow through on promises, and maintain ethical standards to reinforce trust and credibility.

For example, in personal relationships, consistently showing up for loved ones, being reliable in times of need, and honoring commitments strengthen bonds and foster trust. Consistency builds confidence in relationships, creating a stable foundation for mutual support and growth.

Repairing Trust When It's Broken

Trust is fragile and can be disrupted by misunderstandings, breaches of integrity, or conflicts. Effectively repairing trust requires humility, accountability, and a commitment to rebuilding damaged relationships through honest communication and genuine efforts to restore trust.

Acknowledgment and Accountability

Acknowledge the impact of actions or behaviors that led to the breach of trust and take responsibility for their consequences. Demonstrate sincerity and remorse, expressing empathy for the hurt or disappointment caused.

For instance, in professional environments, leaders who acknowledge mistakes, take ownership of errors, and apologize sincerely rebuild trust with stakeholders. Transparency about corrective actions and commitment to ethical conduct restore credibility and foster reconciliation.

Open Communication and Transparency

Open communication and transparency are crucial in repairing trust, as they facilitate honest dialogue, clarify misunderstandings, and rebuild mutual understanding.

Create opportunities for open discussion, listen actively to concerns, and address issues transparently to restore confidence and collaboration.

In interpersonal relationships, openly discussing feelings, concerns, and expectations promotes healing and strengthens emotional bonds. Transparent communication builds trust by demonstrating a willingness to resolve conflicts, learn from mistakes, and nurture mutual respect.

Consistent Efforts and Patience

Repairing trust requires consistent efforts over time to demonstrate reliability, integrity, and genuine commitment to rebuilding relationships. Be patient and understanding of the affected party's emotions, allowing space for healing and rebuilding trust gradually.

For example, in team dynamics affected by a breach of trust, consistent efforts to communicate openly, honor commitments, and demonstrate ethical behavior rebuild credibility and restore confidence among team members. Patience and perseverance in rebuilding trust promote unity, collaboration, and collective success.

Building trust through authentic communication is a transformative process that fosters connection, credibility, and mutual respect in personal and professional relationships. By embracing authenticity in conversations, employing strategies to cultivate trust, and addressing trust repair with humility and transparency, individuals strengthen interpersonal connections and contribute to a positive and supportive social environment. As we navigate the complexities of human relationships, cultivating trust through authentic communication enriches our lives, promotes collaboration, and fosters a culture of empathy, integrity, and mutual understanding.

Chapter 10

Unlocking Meaningful Communication with Anyone

Effective communication forms the bedrock of meaningful connections, transcending boundaries of personality and circumstance to forge bonds of understanding and empathy. We will explore the art of unlocking meaningful communication with anyone, focusing on tailoring approaches to different personalities, fostering genuine interest and curiosity, and harnessing the power of consistent, positive interaction to cultivate lasting relationships and enrich personal interactions.

Tailoring Your Approach to Different Personalities

Every individual possesses a unique blend of traits, preferences, and communication styles that shape how they perceive and engage with the world. Tailoring your communication approach to accommodate diverse personalities enhances rapport, fosters mutual understanding, and facilitates meaningful connections.

Personality Typologies

Understanding personality typologies, such as Myers-Briggs Type Indicator (MBTI) or the Big Five personality traits, provides insights into individuals' behavioral tendencies, preferences, and motivations. Adapt your communication style to resonate with different personality types, adjusting your tone, pace, and approach to suit their preferences.

For instance, extraverted individuals may appreciate engaging conversations and external stimuli, while introverted individuals may prefer deeper, reflective discussions in quieter settings. By tailoring your communication approach to align with their personality traits, you create an environment that promotes comfort, trust, and authentic interaction.

Empathy and Perspective-Taking

Empathy is essential in tailoring your approach to different personalities, as it involves understanding and sharing others' emotions, perspectives, and experiences. Practice perspective-taking by placing yourself in others' shoes, considering their viewpoints, values, and emotional responses to adapt your communication style accordingly.

For example, in professional settings, managers who demonstrate empathy and adaptability in communication build stronger relationships with diverse team members. Acknowledge individual strengths, preferences, and communication styles to foster collaboration, innovation, and mutual respect within teams.

Fostering Genuine Interest and Curiosity

Genuine interest and curiosity form the cornerstone of meaningful communication, reflecting a sincere desire to understand others' experiences, aspirations, and perspectives. Cultivating curiosity enhances engagement, deepens connections, and fosters mutual learning and growth in interpersonal interactions.

Active Listening and Inquiry

Active listening involves fully focusing on others' words, non-verbal cues, and underlying emotions to demonstrate attentiveness and respect. Ask open-ended questions to encourage elaboration and reflection, allowing individuals to share their thoughts, feelings, and insights more freely.

For instance, in personal relationships, asking probing questions about someone's hobbies, interests, or life experiences demonstrates genuine interest and fosters deeper connection. Actively listening and responding with curiosity strengthens emotional bonds and enriches interpersonal relationships.

Sharing Vulnerability and Authenticity

Authentic communication involves sharing vulnerabilities, insecurities, and personal experiences with others, fostering trust, empathy, and emotional connection. By expressing authenticity, individuals create an environment that encourages openness, mutual support, and genuine engagement in conversations.

For example, in group settings, sharing personal stories or challenges can inspire others to share their own experiences, promoting empathy and solidarity. Authenticity cultivates a culture of transparency and vulnerability, enabling individuals to connect on a deeper level and form meaningful relationships based on shared experiences and mutual understanding.

The Power of Consistent and Positive Interaction

Consistent and positive interaction strengthens relationships, builds rapport, and reinforces trust through ongoing engagement and meaningful exchanges.

Harnessing the power of regular interaction cultivates familiarity, strengthens emotional bonds, and sustains meaningful connections over time.

Establishing Regular Communication Routines

Establishing regular communication routines, such as weekly check-ins, coffee meetings, or virtual hangouts, fosters continuity and strengthens relationships. Consistent interaction allows individuals to stay connected, share updates, and provide support, nurturing a sense of belonging and community.

For instance, in professional networks, maintaining regular communication with colleagues, mentors, or industry peers cultivates professional relationships built on trust, collaboration, and mutual respect. Regular interactions create opportunities for knowledge-sharing, mentorship, and career development, enhancing professional growth and success.

Cultivating Positive Communication Habits

Cultivating positive communication habits involves promoting encouragement, appreciation, and constructive feedback in interactions. Acknowledge others' contributions, celebrate achievements, and offer support during challenges to foster a positive and supportive environment.

In personal relationships, expressing gratitude, offering encouragement, and actively celebrating milestones strengthen emotional bonds and nurture enduring connections. Positive communication habits reinforce mutual appreciation, respect, and reciprocity, fostering a climate of positivity and mutual support in relationships.

Unlocking meaningful communication with anyone requires empathy, adaptability, and a commitment to fostering genuine connections built on trust, curiosity, and positive interaction. By tailoring communication approaches to different personalities, cultivating genuine interest and curiosity, and harnessing the power of consistent, positive interaction, individuals enhance their ability to connect authentically, foster empathy, and build enduring relationships across diverse personal and professional contexts. As we navigate the complexities of human interactions, cultivating meaningful communication enriches our lives, promotes understanding, and contributes to a more compassionate and interconnected global community where authentic connections thrive.

Chapter 11

Practical Exercises and Scenarios

Effective communication is not merely a skill but a daily practice that evolves through intentional effort and continuous learning. Here we explore practical exercises and scenarios designed to enhance communication skills, incorporating daily practices, real-life scenarios, role-playing exercises, and self-assessment tools to promote growth, self-awareness, and mastery in interpersonal interactions.

Daily Practices to Improve Communication Skills

Improving communication skills requires consistent practice and reflection to refine techniques, expand capabilities, and adapt to varying contexts and audiences. Incorporating daily practices enhances proficiency, confidence, and effectiveness in verbal and non-verbal communication.

Mindful Communication Exercises

Mindful communication exercises promote present-moment awareness and intentionality in interactions. Practice mindful listening by focusing on the speaker's words, non-verbal cues, and emotional undertones without judgment or distraction. Cultivate mindfulness in communication to enhance empathy, clarity, and connection with others.

For instance, in personal relationships, practice mindful speaking by expressing thoughts and emotions authentically, while remaining attuned to others' responses and reactions. Mindful communication fosters mutual understanding, respect, and emotional connection, nurturing harmonious relationships and deepening interpersonal bonds.

Reflective Journaling

Reflective journaling involves writing down thoughts, experiences, and insights gained from daily interactions to enhance self-awareness and communication skills. Journal about communication challenges, successes, and areas for improvement to identify patterns, strengths, and growth opportunities.

In professional settings, keep a communication journal to document key learnings, effective strategies, and lessons learned from client meetings, presentations, or team collaborations. Reflective journaling promotes continuous learning, personal growth, and refinement of communication techniques to achieve professional success and career advancement.

Real-Life Scenarios and Role-Playing Exercises

Real-life scenarios and role-playing exercises provide practical opportunities to apply communication skills, navigate challenges, and develop adaptive strategies in simulated environments. Engage in role-playing activities to simulate diverse interpersonal scenarios, practice assertiveness, active listening, and conflict resolution techniques.

Scenario-Based Training

Scenario-based training involves creating realistic situations, such as client negotiations, team meetings, or customer interactions, to simulate communication challenges and practice effective responses. Role-play different roles and scenarios to enhance communication agility, decision-making, and problem-solving skills in dynamic environments.

For example, in sales roles, conduct role-playing exercises to practice objection handling, persuasive communication, and customer relationship management.

Role-playing enhances confidence, improvisation skills, and adaptability in navigating diverse client interactions, fostering sales effectiveness and customer satisfaction.

Feedback and Reflection

Feedback and reflection are integral to learning and growth in communication skills, providing insights, perspectives, and constructive criticism to refine techniques and enhance effectiveness. Seek feedback from peers, mentors, or communication coaches to gain valuable insights and identify areas for improvement.

In educational settings, participate in peer feedback sessions to receive constructive criticism, suggestions, and recommendations for enhancing communication clarity, engagement, and impact. Incorporate feedback into practice sessions, role-playing exercises, and real-life scenarios to refine communication strategies and achieve continuous improvement in interpersonal interactions.

Self-Assessment Tools for Continuous Improvement

Self-assessment tools facilitate ongoing evaluation and development of communication skills, enabling individuals to identify strengths, weaknesses, and growth opportunities for personal and professional advancement. Utilize self-assessment tools to gauge communication effectiveness, interpersonal skills, and areas for development.

Communication Style Assessments

Communication style assessments, such as DISC or Insights Discovery, provide insights into individual communication preferences, behaviors, and interaction styles. Complete assessments to understand personal strengths, communication tendencies, and adaptability in diverse social and professional settings.

For instance, in team environments, leverage communication style assessments to enhance collaboration, conflict resolution, and team dynamics. Identify complementary communication styles, leverage strengths, and mitigate potential conflicts to foster synergy, innovation, and productivity within teams.

Goal Setting and Action Planning

Goal setting and action planning facilitate goal alignment, accountability, and progress tracking in communication skills development. Set SMART (Specific, Measurable, Achievable, Relevant, Time-bound) goals for enhancing communication clarity, assertiveness, and emotional intelligence.

In personal development plans, outline specific communication goals, such as improving public speaking skills, enhancing active listening, or mastering non-verbal communication techniques. Create action plans with actionable steps, timelines, and milestones to achieve communication goals effectively and monitor progress over time.

Practical exercises and scenarios offer invaluable opportunities for individuals to enhance communication skills, navigate challenges, and foster continuous improvement in interpersonal interactions. By incorporating daily practices, engaging in real-life scenarios, role-playing exercises, and utilizing self-assessment tools, individuals develop proficiency, confidence, and adaptability in communication across personal and professional contexts. As we embrace the journey of learning and growth in communication skills, we empower ourselves to connect authentically, inspire change, and cultivate meaningful relationships built on trust, empathy, and mutual respect. Embrace the power of practical exercises and scenarios to unlock your full potential in communication and contribute positively to a collaborative, interconnected global community where effective communication thrives.

Chapter 12

Sustaining and Growing Deeper Relationships

Effective communication forms the cornerstone of sustaining and growing deeper relationships, transcending initial connections to foster intimacy, trust, and mutual growth over time. Let us go through long-term strategies for relationship building, cultivating a community of connection, and embracing the journey of lifelong learning in communication to nurture enduring, meaningful relationships.

Long-Term Strategies for Relationship Building

Building and sustaining deeper relationships requires intentional efforts, commitment, and mutual investment in nurturing connections over time. Employ long-term strategies to strengthen bonds, foster trust, and cultivate meaningful interactions that transcend superficial interactions.

Consistent Communication and Engagement

Consistent communication is essential in nurturing deeper relationships, as it demonstrates commitment, reliability, and active engagement in maintaining connections. Prioritize regular check-ins, meaningful conversations, and shared experiences to strengthen emotional bonds and foster mutual understanding.

For instance, in personal relationships, schedule quality time for meaningful conversations, activities, or shared interests to deepen emotional connection and intimacy. Consistent communication promotes trust, empathy, and mutual support, creating a foundation for enduring relationships grounded in respect and authenticity.

Shared Goals and Values

Aligning shared goals and values enhances relationship compatibility and fosters mutual growth and collaboration. Identify common interests, aspirations, and values to cultivate a sense of purpose, direction, and synergy in achieving shared objectives.

In professional collaborations, align team goals, values, and objectives to promote unity, cohesion, and collective success. Establish clear communication channels, foster collaboration, and celebrate achievements to reinforce team cohesion and commitment to shared goals.

Cultivating a Community of Connection

Cultivating a community of connection involves fostering a supportive network of individuals who share common interests, values, and aspirations, promoting collaboration, empathy, and mutual support in personal and professional relationships.

Building Authentic Relationships

Authenticity is integral to cultivating a community of connection, as it fosters trust, transparency, and genuine engagement in interpersonal interactions. Foster authentic relationships by demonstrating sincerity, integrity, and empathy in communication and behavior.

For example, in community settings, participate in networking events, social gatherings, or volunteer opportunities to build authentic relationships based on shared interests and mutual respect. Authentic connections nurture a sense of belonging, support, and camaraderie, enriching personal and professional relationships.

Empowering Others and Promoting Inclusivity

Empowering others and promoting inclusivity foster a sense of belonging, acceptance, and collaboration within

96

communities. Encourage diverse perspectives, celebrate cultural diversity, and embrace inclusivity to create an environment that values and respects individuals' unique contributions and experiences.

In organizational cultures, promote inclusivity through inclusive leadership practices, diversity initiatives, and equitable opportunities for professional growth and development. Empower team members to voice their ideas, perspectives, and concerns, fostering a culture of innovation, creativity, and collective success.

The Journey of Lifelong Learning in Communication

Lifelong learning in communication is a continuous process of self-discovery, growth, and adaptation to evolving interpersonal dynamics, communication technologies, and societal changes. Embrace the journey of lifelong learning to enhance communication proficiency, deepen relationships, and navigate challenges with resilience and empathy.

Continuous Skill Development

Continuous skill development involves acquiring new knowledge, refining communication techniques, and adapting strategies to enhance effectiveness and relevance in diverse contexts. Pursue ongoing education, training, or professional development opportunities to broaden skills, expand perspectives, and stay abreast of industry trends.

For instance, in professional environments, attend workshops, seminars, or online courses to develop advanced communication skills, such as negotiation, conflict resolution, or cross-cultural communication. Continuous skill development empowers individuals to navigate complex challenges, foster innovation, and achieve professional excellence.

Reflection and Self-Assessment

Reflection and self-assessment are critical in lifelong learning, as they promote self-awareness, identify strengths and areas for improvement, and facilitate personal growth and development. Engage in reflective practices, journaling, or peer feedback to gain insights into communication effectiveness and adaptability.

In personal growth journeys, reflect on communication experiences, challenges, and successes to cultivate self-awareness and refine interpersonal skills. Self-assessment encourages accountability, goal setting, and continuous improvement in communication practices, fostering resilience, adaptability, and lifelong learning.

Sustaining and growing deeper relationships through effective communication requires dedication, empathy, and a commitment to nurturing connections over time. By employing long-term strategies for relationship building, cultivating a community of connection, and embracing the journey of lifelong learning in communication, individuals strengthen emotional bonds, foster collaboration, and contribute to a supportive, interconnected global community where meaningful relationships thrive. As we navigate the complexities of human interactions, cultivate relationships grounded in authenticity, empathy, and mutual respect to enrich lives, inspire change, and foster a culture of unity and collaboration. Embrace the journey of sustaining and growing deeper relationships through effective communication to create a lasting legacy of connection, understanding, and shared prosperity in personal and professional relationships alike.

Conclusion

In exploring the future of human connection, we embark on a journey that transcends the boundaries of time and space, studying deep into the essence of what it means to connect authentically in an ever-evolving world. This conclusion serves as a beacon, guiding us through the profound insights gained from mastering conversations, understanding the transformative impact of genuine connections on personal and professional lives, and envisioning a future where communication trends shape our interactions.

Embracing the Journey of Mastering Conversations

At the heart of every meaningful connection lies the art of mastering conversations. It is not merely about the exchange of words but the ability to listen deeply, understand empathetically, and respond thoughtfully. Throughout this journey, we have explored the intricate layers of communication—practical, emotional, and social—learning that each layer contributes uniquely to the tapestry of human relationships.

Mastering practical conversations involves clarity, conciseness, and effective information exchange. It is about conveying thoughts and ideas with precision while ensuring understanding and alignment of objectives. Whether in personal relationships or professional settings, mastering practical conversations lays the groundwork for clear expectations, efficient problem-solving, and collaborative decision-making.

Emotional conversations delve into the depths of human experience, navigating feelings, vulnerabilities, and empathy. It requires not only the ability to express emotions authentically but also to empathize with others' emotional landscapes. In personal relationships, emotional conversations foster intimacy, trust, and mutual support, strengthening bonds and deepening connections. In professional contexts, emotional intelligence in conversations enhances leadership, team dynamics, and organizational culture, fostering a climate of empathy, respect, and psychological safety.

Social conversations encompass the broader context of societal norms, cultural nuances, and interpersonal dynamics. It involves understanding social cues, adapting to diverse environments, and fostering inclusive interactions. Mastering social conversations empowers individuals to navigate social complexities, build rapport, and forge meaningful connections across cultural and geographical boundaries.

The Impact of Genuine Connection on Personal and Professional Life

Genuine connection transcends transactional exchanges; it embodies authenticity, trust, and mutual respect. In personal life, genuine connections enrich our emotional well-being, providing a sense of belonging, support, and companionship. It fosters resilience during challenging times, celebrates joys, and creates lasting memories that enrich the tapestry of our lives.

In professional life, genuine connections drive collaboration, innovation, and organizational success. It enhances teamwork, communication, and collective problem-solving capabilities within teams and across departments. Leaders who prioritize genuine connections inspire loyalty, motivation, and commitment among employees, fostering a positive work environment where individuals thrive and contribute to shared goals with passion and dedication.

The impact of genuine connections extends beyond individual relationships; it shapes organizational culture, customer relationships, and stakeholder engagement. Businesses that prioritize genuine connections with customers build brand loyalty, advocacy, and sustainable growth. It fosters trust and credibility, positioning organizations as trusted partners that prioritize customer satisfaction and long-term relationships.

Looking Ahead: Evolving with Communication Trends

As we look towards the future, the landscape of communication continues to evolve with technological advancements, cultural shifts, and global connectivity. Embracing these trends requires adaptability, innovation, and a commitment to lifelong learning in communication. Virtual platforms, artificial intelligence, and digital communication tools reshape how we connect, collaborate, and engage with others, offering new opportunities for global connectivity and inclusive dialogue.

The future of human connection lies in harnessing technology to enhance, rather than replace, genuine human interactions. It calls for integrating empathy, authenticity, and ethical considerations into digital communications to foster meaningful connections and uphold human values in a digital age. Embracing these evolving communication trends empowers individuals and organizations to stay agile, responsive, and connected in an interconnected world.

Moreover, looking ahead entails addressing emerging challenges and opportunities in communication, such as navigating digital etiquette, managing information overload, and fostering inclusive dialogue across diverse cultural and generational perspectives. It requires proactive measures to promote digital literacy, ethical communication practices, and responsible use of technology to mitigate risks and maximize the benefits of digital connectivity.

The future of human connection is shaped by our collective commitment to mastering conversations, nurturing genuine connections, and embracing communication trends that enhance our interactions. By prioritizing authenticity, empathy, and mutual respect in every conversation, we cultivate meaningful relationships that transcend barriers, bridge differences, and foster a sense of belonging in a rapidly changing world.

As we navigate the complexities of human interactions, let us continue to embrace the transformative power of genuine connections in personal and professional life. Let us celebrate diversity, cultivate empathy, and foster inclusive dialogue that promotes understanding and unity across communities and cultures. Together, we embark on a journey towards a future where human connection thrives, empowered by our ability to listen deeply, speak thoughtfully, and connect authentically with others.

The future of human connection is not just a destination but an ongoing evolution—a journey of growth, understanding, and shared experiences that enrich our lives and shape the world we live in. Let us embrace this journey with optimism, resilience, and a commitment to building a more connected, compassionate, and inclusive global community where every conversation matters and every connection makes a difference.

www.ingramcontent.com/pod-product-compliance
Lightning Source LLC
Chambersburg PA
CBHW071938210526
45479CB00002B/736